I0186669

HUMAN LANDSCAPE

Published by Dreaming Deer Press
Marietta, GA, USA 30067

Copyright © 2018 by Joseph S. Plum
All rights reserved.

ISBN-13: 9780692636237

ISBN-10: 0692636234

No portion of this book may be reproduced without prior written permission from the publisher, except brief selections for reviews or articles.

Cover art by Emily Lupita, watercolor & ink, 2004.

Printed in the United States of America

For poetry books, CDs & DVDs
by Joseph S. Plum, please visit:

www.JoePlum.com

Human Landscape

Joseph S. Plum

Dreaming Deer Press

Preface

The poems written in this book were transcribed from the original oral poetry that was crafted in the bardic tradition of dreaming and living a lifetime in connection with nature. The hope is that by writing down the poems and collecting them into books, they may travel widely and be shared with the world. If you have a chance, please say these poems aloud. In this way, the beauty and power of traditional bardic poetry will live on through your voice.

Artist's Statement

rain is what will become of me

one last chance to wash away dusty sovereignty

and return to this conscious stream

dreams of childhood immortality

released from the structured confines

of their thoughtful cages!

-Joseph Samuel Plum

from *phantom*

Contents

for Fire

moonlit children

greetings from the starlight tribes
clans of midnight
i am an American Bard
a native bardic poet
speaking for the land
my function is manifold
yet somewhat singular
today, like many days
because we choose it
we are taking part
in a dangerous revolution
for bardic poetry is as revolutionary
as it is dangerous
for bardic poetry is like the kiss of a lover
to one who has half-forgotten love
at once unexpected, always terrifying
yet somehow sweet and entrancing
full of beauty and wonder when first it comes
it comes!
but then it goes
oh, how it goes!

and darkness follows

a leaping sadness in the heart

a questing unfulfilled

a long, strange, aching stillness

which wraps us inside

if you are honest

prepare

prepare now

to ask yourself

"what is this fine breath of air?"

    between the place of living

and the place of dying

i have been walking

past the point of stemming

i have traveled

inbound on the northern tides

through the portal of the regal eyes

wrapped in memory's disguise

within the touch of the white one

my sun soul has arrived

    in the dream silence

the embers keep glowing

though the flame is extinguished

smoke is still rising

while in the high heavens

the star sisters are watching

for the moonlit children to come dancing

through great clouds that are climbing

into a sky laced with soft fingers

eagerly stretching towards the pale light

of a gentler good morning

    and the moonlit children

are talented in ways

not given to nations

or secured in days

and they can feel

a partition in the mind

a blockage of jumbled thoughts

of kin and kind

through which sweeps

a cool, life giving air

a sweeter breeze

for a once darker fare

(hand holds on that sovereign chair).

    who lingers?

half-sleeping in soft repose

or passing among temples of a distant time

or seeking unseen some future sign

what is this fine breath of air?

this ageless gift from we know not where

this sightless path scented

with honey vapor of silken tongue.

    if it pleases the gods

may it be a truth

that love and destiny

are one.

human landscape

if you wish
i shall sing for you
a song of bright enchantment,
i will weave a web
of silver strand
and call to mind
enlightened innocence
with which you may travel free
across this gracious land,
but first
you must work
against the veil
of dark attachment
you must draw back
the curtain
with a steady
yet unseen hand
you must conceive
in the soul's
direct advancement
by believing in words

that only the heart

can understand.

    for in this time

of lost remembrances

where the greater dream

forgets the lesser man

we are all in danger

of living out our lives

as shadows

bound up and blinded

then flattened

by the contours

of what these

surface worlds demand.

    that is why

when i am old

i want to stand

on emotion's edge

when the first storms

of the season have come

to beat the land

with one hundred thousand

miles of wind

just like a giant fist
on a mighty drum.
     that is why
when i leave this earth
it will be
beneath the foaming wave
of a roaring sea
to merge again
with the ancient currents
of a surging faith
that have for so long
crisscrossed inside of me.
     someday
i shall fall asleep
on the rising tide
with salt and sand
in my hair
when i wake again
on the other side
i know i'll find
both an angel
and a devil
waiting there.

        earthly music

quickly becomes

just so much noise

without the proper harmonies

to make the rhythms clear.

that is why to choose

the place and day

your ego dies

will draw the host

of heaven near.

        many times

i myself

have been drawn

to clouds folded

on the horizon

only to find

that they were mountains

with giants sleeping

and breathing

inside them

if you come to stand

on the edge

of the high plains of creation

the vista

which opens up above

holds no need

for explanation.

    drop your burdens

in the valley

leave your reasons

among the people below

climb the peaks

carrying only your courage

to speak

with the ancient ones

who can truly show

how to turn

this world into feeling,

and feeling into world

thereby revealing

an understanding

whose meaning

is likened unto a pearl

for all around

an internal irritation

undigested memories grow

secreting a wealth of being

that few of us

if any

ever come to know,

until high on a ridge

dividing joy from sorrows

where the cross winds of eternity

never cease to blow

there through a swinging gate

of no tomorrows

the timeless pathways

of vital energies flow

crossing themselves

in awe and wonder

as a momentary void

intersects an infinite plane

weaving us in unison

with a moment of splendor

after which no one

is ever quite the same.

rise up and step

into the larger arena

circle

with the movement of the sun

pull

your hands together

in a gesture of prayer

for every one.

    prepare

to enter the instant

for in no time at all

you'll find

the spirit of life has come

then all that is left

to be brought into balance

the angels will do

once our journey is done.

    when for you

the night sky becomes

a foreign country

as the ground air

begins to cool,

and the poor beg you

take all our possessions!

while the rich pray

no, make it my most precious jewel.

then for you

the traveler within

must take up with another

in order to please

the guards

waiting at the border line

for to pass into the threshold

of that realm of no dominion

takes a fresh

and portable sacrifice

each and every time.

    when the angels come

to build

their city in the clouds

with the hope

that you'll be there

even though

your body lies still

stretched out upon the ground

in aching, unspeakable despair

know now

that your spirit shall rise

with the morning mist

to kiss

the sun warmed air

while those who beat

and tear at their breast

must go elsewhere

to insist they truly care.

if human beings are battlefields

then we must become overgrown with weeds

so all the bodies that have died

but were never buried

can turn now into flowers

who will someday

be dropping all their seeds.

for if the sun is rising

to chase away the dark

then very soon

the inner earth will again be warming

as these clouds of blindness

begin to part

and the gods of war

who have been forever fighting

shall find a new conflict

visited upon their hearts

a conquest

whose struggles end in silence

alone

amid their own world's

highest mountain tops.

    by living

in a human landscape

with choices to be made

the price

of healing wounded innocence

is never quite completely paid

unless the geometry of the situation

grows honestly

from a matrix

born of instinctive faith

so that the opportunity

to strike a reflex blow

in the name of glory

can without hesitation

be ultimately allowed

to escape.

very here of forever

child of mine
be the seed
that always flowers
bear the fruits of time
be this moment becoming hours
ripen on the vine
be the sweet that never sours
throttle back your mind
be the voice of ancient powers
carry on this rhyme
be the children
who are the children
born of the promise
that was given
in the gardens of mankind
you are a ballet of shadows
a dance of lights
an earthly landscape
of endless insights
you are a sense of being
living in this time of becoming

you are a deep well of feeling

feeding an oasis of homecoming.

  an offhand notion

awaits to disclose

an umbilical chord of emotion

that when traveled flows

outward through a heart of devotion

to become a tear in the eyes of those

who have just crossed over

from that mother ocean

into this fragile land

where each new vista shows

another kingdom full of fairy tales

ripe with a wealth of stories to be told

in just such a way

that the child within us knows

what lesson it is

this new fable holds

and why the path of understanding

always takes us down that road alone

so as to lead us

through a wilderness of civilization

to where one day - someday

every child of time must go

to stand there on the banks

of a mighty river of realization

in whose waters

the current continues to expose

a seedbed of language

spawned in the sediments of old

an archaic inclination

overtaken during germination

by the context of the whole

reappearing only after incubation

as a deepening appreciation

of the emerging articulation

of unexpressed feeling

where in we as we know us

first began to unfold

rolling like a thunder that is echoing

down the sunlit slopes of a valley

worth remembering

where we are all children

alive and growing

in the homeland of our souls

where throughout the ages

that are assembling

from the source of all beginnings

a newborn sense is stirring

to a voice

which dresses in the dawning

and begins again to journey

in a light that speaks of morning

towards a future

which holds the coming present

until the present comes

wrapped in a sunrise that is a remnant

of a time when we were one

with a season that has been immortalized

in the singing of ten thousand lullabies

which have just now reached us here

in one final push to make it clear

that our last awakening is so very near

    in this land of sleeping butterflies

child like infant caterpillars cry

with the hope that we'll be there

listening in answer to their prayer

that's asking us to hear

revelations encased in our inner ear

visions that come clothed

in silken words which appear

spinning cocoons

around every drop of air

while whispering

that this is where

the very here of forever

becomes apparent

by giving birth to the here and now

in fulfillment of our ancestors

most sacred vow

that delivers in the offspring of tomorrow

this message of old

as an inborn tongue of silver

calls out to a heart of gold

"child of mine

bring forth into this world

that is ours

a quality divine

by giving to the future

that is yours

the spirit parents of mankind

who are of one voice

that is calling

now

now is the time

to be a child

to do the telling

to be a child of time."

cast off

there is a season
cast off from scientific sorcery
where blindness is broken
by imagery
where the epitome of ecstasy
illuminates all eternity
there the face of the future
has eyes to see
right into the very heart of me
for once the essential can be seen
beauty comes in between
a moment of awakening
and a lifetime of living
what once was a dream.

carved in stone
etched in bone
embracing each other
we feel our way home
like young gods
with old promises to keep
with a heart full of longing

we search the faces we meet

for a glimpse of belonging

to that eternal echo

which will always repeat

in a tongue that is ancient

and a voice which is sweet

a rhyme of returning

to the earth at our feet

in the hopes of reclaiming

the balance we need

in order to regain

the momentum

the speed

which gives us the ability

to both follow and lead

until escape velocity

is finally achieved,

that the clarity of our vision

may once more be freed

from the weight of our understanding

and the gravity of our greed.

words of proud possession
make us what we are
while the echoing of our voices
drowns the twinkling of the stars
our duty is our master
our master makes us slaves
chains our ears to our tongues
leads us to the grave
on that day
that life is through with us
when all we do is not enough
after what we have is given up
maybe then we'll find ourselves
maybe then we'll see
that words of proud possession
will never set us free
and our duty
which was done so well
can never let us be.

usefulness

my usefulness amazes me
it brands me on my feet
burns like fire on my flesh
and then condemns me to repeat
the mournful cries of industrious lives
whose workings never cease
for as long as i live
to see myself in other men's eyes
when none of them are me

yes, my usefulness amazes me
bends my back and shapes my hands
then taunts me with the hope of being free
takes up the blade every day
and uses it oh so skillfully
to cut the beating heart right out of me
while pushing away
the open arms
of a breathless, waiting eternity
yes, usefulness
amazes
(me).

the language of birds

there is a secret
i will always keep
until there is no one
to keep it from
for there is a message
i shall never speak
until long after
i've lost this tongue
i know
another voice somewhere
will rise up
beneath the setting sun
and give this earth
its closing prayer
in a language
and a scripture
from a time
that's yet to come
    grant to me
the free born air
filled with a wind

that will rattle, thunder, and drum

to draw close

those who can truly share

even though

they be deaf

blind and dumb

spirits

need not ears to hear

nor eyes

to see their way clear

to enter our hearts

make a home there

with room enough to care

for this dream that awakens

through both dark and light

that they and theirs

might sleep to be here

among the margins of any body

with no reason to alarm

or treasures

to guard out of fear

    yes, there is a secret

I shall forever keep

there is no telling

what i found

emerging out of chaos

and confusion

backwards and upside down

yes there is a secret

learned long ago

as the shorebirds

who were poets

flew away

while calling back to me

over their shoulder wings

with a cry

which seemed to say

"tomorrow

when we meet again

as promised

in the service

of the coming day

bring with you

the thunder at twilight

to silence

all the spirits

singing on the way

then together

we shall gather

their shadows around us

even as the quiet

begins to fade

that with blood

and dust

and feathered air

a platform for leaping

can be made

for it is only

with the language of birds

the shadows of spirits

and an open heart

that the foundations

of a future age

will be laid

as it is the mixing

of these essential elements

with one other lost ingredient

that this world of ours

shall

from the human race

be saved."

cloud mountain

and so it is
that the mountain
comes to the cloud
and cloud to the mountain
for mountain is ancestor to the cloud
and cloud
child of the parents' breath
and breath
force and will of spirit
and spirit
fire and vapor of life

to fill the oceans
empty your mind
to cleanse the heart
calibrate time
to instruct the eye
open the soul

    to cradle
this one single moment
of homecoming
just let go!

magic undone

it was magic that's what i'll say

it was magic which took my heart away

it was magic i know i'm right

it was magic and not the night

that came to call cold and still

to enter my blood and drink its fill

to take my breath and cast a spell

which works from inside to make me ill

to lock me up while i grow old

to grind and twist what once was whole

to separate me from my very soul

it was magic that's what i say

it was magic which came my way

it was magic i know i'm right

it was magic and not the night.

how long has it been since that fateful day

when a magical moment led me astray

where is the one to set me right

to put back in my chest what i lost that night

to take me and hold me tight

to never give up the will to fight

an unseen enemy who can't be known

an enchanted army that's forever reborn

from a world of sorrowful winds and emotional storms

where among the sons and daughters of men

a long and unused path winds its way home

    it was magic, that's what i say

it was magic which came, then went away

i'd almost forgotten what magic can do

i'd almost forgotten that i'm magic too!

the frozen lands

in these hands
there sleeps a musician
whose instrument
has never been made,
a composer of songs
which will not be played,
the keeper of melody
whose harmonies are being saved
for a performance of release
from the shallows of an earthly grave.

in this heart there is a fire
whose spark shall remain
even after being swallowed
by the confines of that eternal flame,
and where the ashes are each spread
long after the warmth has all fled,
in the air there is a voice
which will rise up
and breathe life into words
that have never before been said.

yes, there is a dispeller of night

in this world of the spiritually dead,

a bringer of sunlight

to these frozen lands

whose ice once fed

springs that would turn to rivers,

to wash away dark blindness

from these eyes in our heads,

tears to mirror dreams of great price,

asleep in our beds.

    in this life

many a time we have acted

like children of the material gods,

those who by thinking

thought they could conquer

the unbeatable odds.

we have been youthful spirits

with no clan to protect or profess,

we have been infants without angels

who would guard us and then bless.

    although we are bound

to the body,

still we have eyes

that gaze skyward.

by searching the heavens

with no thought for reward

while keeping an ear to this earth,

an enchanting duet

of musical debate can be heard.

for what the gods in their wisdom

proclaim as being absolute,

my great mother in her laughter

calls absurd.

salt water call

flowing out
across rough waters
beneath a cloud formed
from the tears of the mist dawn mother
down to this river
come the whirlwind whispers
beating to a froth
waves of voices inside of me
saying green are the pastures
that feed the fishes of the sea
black is the drink
of tomorrow's wishes
clear to the bottom
of yesterday's riches
where silver is the fog
about to fall
between rains in the delta
where the water tastes
of upstream, midstream, and all
except for that moment
when the currents lie still

and the wind blows backward
with the saltwater call

    "child" it whispers
"child stand tall"
all children are born knowing
which way to crawl
yet one day walking
starts with a stumble
then running with a fall
child come quickly
the clouds await
welcome to the ocean
every young raindrop's fate.

fundamental lesson

there is a beauty in winter
children often see
head down in the snow, lost
in the whiteness of an endless sea.
there is a vision set in the cold
old bones sometimes ignore
face up in a dream afraid
morning will come no more.
but for those few who are ageless
winter holds a virtue deep,
a taste for life long after
colors are asleep.
with an eye for light and shadow
bountifully released
hearts can dance
with the echo of eternity at peace.
yes, there is a beauty in winter,
a promise which will always keep
the seeds of spring's awakening
safe within tomorrow's reach.
for fertile ground when frozen

humbles honor with icy speech

and that the truth

is fundamentally ultimate

still stands as the one lesson

only winter's stark beauty

has the power to teach.

two suns rising
(if only I could stand)

     raven tongued

back bent skyward

sudden illness come morning

a small sun rises

beneath great hills

clouds

that would billow

     a star once brazen

now grown ashen

to be swallowed

by swirling mountains above

two crows

black flying black

dip decided

touch land

walk

heads bent

inspect

this distant window

      drifting

no anchor

no bounds

small sounds stir

blanketed in warmth

still chills run to perch

near the tips of a hand

      talk

travels soft

sinks deep into the heart

where beneath roofboard ribs

of this quiet house

all day long with the wind

walls shake.

desert years

a painter of deserts
labored for years
laying grain upon grain
and tear upon tear
before the sun rose
and after the moon fell
he struggled not to struggle
or drop into hell
finally the artist had finished
and he knew he'd done well
for around him stretched
the mountains of sand
all that had sprung
from the tips of his hand
all that he'd lost
and all that he'd found
reached up to meet him
and it pulled him down
as the ground rushed
to greet him
with a sigh

and a thud

he tore his heart

and he lost his blood

which flowed across

the endless sand

to fill the portrait

that the painter

called man

    now the painter's been gone

for many a year

though his paints and his brushes

both are still here

begin in the middle

end at the start

trust in your luck

and follow your heart

when you do this with ease

you've done your part

to give to yourself

what can't be taught

the talent to turn

everyday life

into a work of art.

children of the sun

soundly driven inward

iron waves of memory

rush upon me

bringing twisted roots of promise

full into view

the fruit of every flower

holds a seed of returning

nurtured without a hope

watered by a sigh

fashioned after a dream

half the distance of an angel's wing

flicks across my eye

leaving unchanged the hearts

of those who are called

once to be reborn

walking on the edge of remembering

never have i seen a day so full

stand on the shores of forever

listen as the story unfolds

sit around the fire at sunset

talk of this life which we know

once upon a time there was nothing

no where or no way to grow old

but now that we're suddenly

about to be children again

is it here that tomorrow will find us

here at the edge of our souls?

    yes, the time has come

for the children of the sun

to take shelter on the water

yes the time has come for everyone

for all the sons and daughters

so come stand by me

if you're ready to leave

if you hear the voices calling

through the window at night

or in the morning light

do you feel the tide a falling

yes the time has come

for every lost one

to take shelter on the water

for out there in the seas afloat

in a storm, there's a hope

a home with the promise

of a father, a mother,
a sister, a brother.
    yes the time has come
for the children of the sun
to begin a journey
that's like no other!

tidal river delta
(so long to myself)

outside these windows

there is a battle going on

echoing reflections

for the unknown

shadows of shadows

are waking in a dream

to find themselves

not as they seem

scattered inside

a cosmos of souls

broken promises

strive to be whole

searching among

armies of wind

for a breath of still air

in which to begin

gathering a storm

of words to send

to wash out the mouths

of mortal men

that they might speak

with the force

of nature again
    if i could create
i would compose
a written letter
to say a word
to give a meaning
to a voice unheard
to bring about
a miraculous birth
to begin a wind
that will sweep this earth
to set each foot
down on the path
to make again round
what once was flat
to separate what is this
from what was that
    in a dream
your earth was my sky
and what for you was low
was for me high
and when you walked
upon your ground
above my head
came a thunderous sound

if you should seek

to be with me here

know that

what for you is far

is for me near

    given the breath

and the tongue

that it takes

i express with silence

why my heart aches

to part the sky

to swim in the ground

to keep the secret

of the promise i found

there is so much

to honestly feel

to clothe my emptiness

in what is real

to embrace with tenderness

a lifetime of bliss

to deliver to you

with my eyes

this thinly veiled abyss

which gathers in my blood

like some primordial mist

descended from the hilltops

and the mountain cliffs

always carrying within it

the most precious of gifts

which gives to us all

what each of us would miss

the kiss of life

to moisten our lips

a conception of light

in total eclipse

with the birth of a word

which allows us to see

a world where truth

is completely free

to reveal a beauty

which helps us believe

in a time existing endlessly

in harmony

with a melody

that is the heartbeat

of eternity

   do not of the past

or of the future be

speak not of this

if you talk of me
for the day is coming
when you will know
that in hearing goodbye
i'm saying hello.

About the Author

Joseph Samuel Plum is a direct descendant of Welsh bards and Native American spirit. He lives in South Central Iowa within a group of trees where he composes and presents bardic poetry of original nature. He has been doing this for fifty years. This is his sixth book.

Books by Joseph S. Plum

RELICS

CONCENTRIC DEVOTION

LANDMASS AND OTHER POEMS

STAR SIGHT GATHERING

WHERE RISING VOICES GROW

HUMAN LANDSCAPE

NOBLE REMNANTS

BOOK OF SHADOWS

OLD PATH

www.JoePlum.com

www.ingramcontent.com/pod-product-compliance
Lightning Source LLC
Chambersburg PA
CBHW051708090426
42736CB00013B/2605